The Golden Eagle

Michael Everett

MICHAEL EVERETT was a keen amateur birdwatcher from 1952 to 1964. In the latter year he joined the staff of the R.S.P.B. in Edinburgh and became involved in all aspects of the Society's work in Scotland. This included the Golden Eagle Survey and 'Operation Osprey' at Loch Garten. During his time in Scotland he developed an interest in birds of prey in general and eagles in particular.

Since 1969 he has worked at the R.S.P.B. headquarters in Bedfordshire as Assistant Reserves Manager, and he is also closely concerned with special protection jobs—mainly with birds of prey.

Michael Everett is a contributor to the R.S.P.B. magazine, *Birds,* and to various scientific journals. He is the author of *Birds of Prey* and *A Natural History of Owls.*

Cover illustration: Female eagle at the nest

THE GOLDEN EAGLE

Michael Everett

Photographs by C. E. Palmar

WILLIAM BLACKWOOD
1977

First published in 1977 by
William Blackwood & Sons Ltd
32 Thistle Street
Edinburgh EH2 1HA
Scotland

ISBN 0 85158 119 6

Printed at the Press of
the Publisher

Contents

Illustrations

INTRODUCTION   If Scotland were to choose a national bird, I imagine that the Golden Eagle would emerge as odds-on favourite for the title. It is hard to think of any other bird which is so essentially Scottish, even if it is not so very long ago since it made a brief comeback in Ulster and has now started to nest again in England. Actually, fewer than twenty species of birds breed in Scotland and nowhere else in the British Isles. Very few of them, with the notable exception of the Osprey, are at all well known outside ornithological circles, and indeed most of them can be seen outside Scotland either as migrants or winter visitors. The Osprey probably gains more publicity than any other British bird and has almost become the unofficial symbol of the conservation movement in Scotland, while the little Crested Tit has a place of its own as the emblem of the Scottish Ornithologists' Club. I know both birds quite well and they would certainly rank high on a personal list of favourites, but to me the Golden Eagle is *the* Scottish bird.

Fortunately, Scotland's eagle population is still large and widespread and, notwithstanding the threats it faces in some areas, it seems to be a fairly healthy one. It is no exaggeration to say that the population is one of the largest and most important in Europe. Scottish eagles are among the most thoroughly studied birds of prey in the world, and Scottish studies have formed the foundations for much of the work done elsewhere in Europe and in the U.S.A. during the last twenty years or so.

Even so, a great mythology still surrounds the Golden Eagle, as occasional articles in the more sensational newspapers show all too clearly. The big birds are often misunderstood and grossly misrepresented; they are often disliked by their human neighbours and as a result are often heavily persecuted. In this book I hope to show the Golden Eagle as it really is, and also to show that it is a bird we should be proud of. As I think you will see, even when all the fantasy

1

is swept aside, the Golden Eagle remains a fascinating and rather special bird.

In some ways this is a highly personal account in which I have recorded some of my own observations and points of view. Nevertheless, in writing it I have drawn freely on the published work of many colleagues and eagling friends, for no one person should claim to be able to say the last word on this remarkable bird. Any errors of fact or interpretation are mine, not theirs.

MEET THE GOLDEN EAGLE Drawing up a precise definition of an eagle has baffled the world's foremost experts on birds of prey. There are about sixty species of eagles in the world, ranging from very large and impressively powerful birds down to others which are smaller than our own Common Buzzard. Indeed, with some species the dividing line between eagles and Buzzards and other big hawks is very blurred. Sheer size and strength and special powers of flight do not necessarily make an eagle! If all the eagles were like the Golden Eagle and its close relatives there would be no problem: at least there can be no doubt about the identity of these birds. For the purposes of this book it will be sufficient to compare our bird with some of its closest relatives before moving on to look at it in more detail. Readers interested in finding out more about other eagles are referred to the Reading List on page 60.

The Golden Eagle is grouped with eight or nine other eagles in the genus *Aquila* and is one of a larger number of birds known collectively as the 'true' or 'booted' eagles—the latter name referring to the fact that their legs are feathered down to the base of the toes and are not bare as in other birds of prey. In the system of scientific nomenclature we use today, each species has a two-word Latin title which is unique and precludes confusion with any other species. This avoids the difficulties of using only vernacular names, which can be identical but mean quite different things in different countries. For example, our Robin is a very different bird

2

from the Robin of North America. The first of the two Latin words, in this case *Aquila* ('eagle'), is the name of the genus in which closely related species are grouped together. The second word, which is adjectival, means nothing on its own, but when it is added to the first it produces the unique species name. Thus, the Golden Eagle is *Aquila chrysaetos*, the second word being a Latinised form of two Greek words, *khrusos*—gold—and *aetos*—eagle. Among its relatives in the same genus, the Imperial Eagle becomes *Aquila heliaca*, the Spotted Eagle *Aquila clanga*—and so on.

Most of the *Aquila* eagles are birds of plains, open country or even wooded habitats. This is true of the Imperial Eagle and the two species of Spotted Eagle in Europe, for example—none of these is a mountain eagle. Although the Golden Eagle does occur on open plains in some regions, it is, throughout its world-wide range, essentially an upland bird, associated with mountains in most places. In some countries, including Scotland, it occurs down to sea-level and may even breed along the coast. The only other true mountain eagle in the *Aquila* group is the handsome Black or Verreaux's Eagle which replaces our bird in Africa south of the Sahara.

As the photographs in this book show, the Golden Eagle is a large and handsomely proportioned bird—but since a lot of nonsense is talked about its size and wingspan it might be as well to settle the bird's vital statistics at the outset. We will come back to the question of physical strength later. A full-grown eagle measures 30 to 36 ins from bill-tip to tail-tip, males being at the smaller end of the scale and females much larger—another phenomenon we shall come back to. A male's wingspan is between 6 ft 2 ins and 7 ft, usually averaging 6 ft 7 ins, and that of the female is between 7 ft and 7 ft 5 ins, averaging around 7 ft 2½ ins. Large females have been recorded with spans of 8 ft, but these are very exceptional. European males may weigh as little as 6¾ lb, or as much as 9¾ lb, but usually average around 8½ lb; the range for females is 8¾ lb to nearly 13 lb, but an average weight is about 10¼ lb. American birds have very similar measurements and weights, but some from north-east Asia tend to be rather larger.

IDENTIFICATION   Many bird books have excellent pictures of eagles at rest, but in practice most birdwatchers will see the Golden Eagle in flight and often at a distance, so here we will concentrate on identifying the flying eagle. However, a basic plumage description is necessary first. Essentially, Golden Eagles are big, more or less uniformly brown birds, only very slightly darker on the back and wings. Immature birds tend to be much darker than adults, but among the latter there is a great deal of individual variation: very dark and relatively pale eagles are not uncommon. The most famous feature of the bird (and one of the most difficult to see well in the field) is the pale, straw-coloured feathering on the crown and the nape of the neck which gives it its English name. In some lights this area can look really golden, but in very bright conditions it can also look almost white. The bill is blackish, with the bare cere at its base yellow. The feet, which can often be seen well when the bird is in flight are also yellow. At a distance the eye looks uniformly dark, but at close range shows a hazel-coloured iris, paler in adults than in immatures.

On the wing, an adult eagle appears as a very large and rather dark bird, even looking wholly black at great distances; sometimes the uniform plumage is broken by slightly paler bases to the flight-feathers and tail-feathers. Seen from above, it may show large pale 'shoulder-patches' where the wing-coverts contrast strongly with the darker flight-feathers. No Golden Eagle ever shows the contrasting patterns of the underwing and underparts which are characteristic of many Buzzards. Immature eagles have two very obvious features, striking in their first year of life and becoming progressively less conspicuous as they grow older until they disappear altogether in the fourth or fifth year. These are conspicuous white flashes at the bend of the wing (the carpal joint), rather more obvious on the underwing, and a white base to the otherwise dark tail. An immature eagle in

4

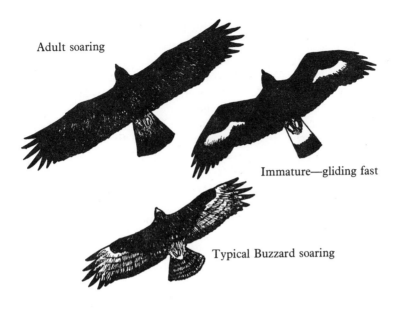

Adult soaring

Immature—gliding fast

Typical Buzzard soaring

Eagle soaring—profile

Buzzard soaring—profile

Distant immature

Distant adult

Flight identification

this plumage can hardly be confused with any other large bird of prey, and indeed the white in the wings and tail can be seen very easily, even at very long range. The Rough-legged Buzzard, a rare winter visitor to Scotland, has a similar tail pattern, but lacks the white in the wings and in any case is typically a very pale bird below.

Seen at reasonably close range, a Golden Eagle is not too hard to identify. Size alone often clinches the matter. However, even observers who spend a lot of time in eagle country do not see the bird close to all that often and for practical purposes we have to think in terms of rather more subtle aids to identification.

An eagle is so big that it can be seen more than a mile away with the naked eye and can be picked up at much greater distances through binoculars. At such extreme range, and even in the 'middle distance', some of the plumage features referred to above might not be seen very well, especially in indifferent light, and it can be very hard to assess the bird's size with any accuracy. So the outline of an eagle becomes all-important, as does its actual mode of flight; the latter very much affects the former. Eagles move with heavy, powerful flaps and short glides, usually when covering short distances or moving around crags. Sometimes the speed of these wing-beats can be very deceptive, suggesting a much smaller bird, but more often in my experience the typical, deep, leisurely beat can convey an impression of power shared by no other large raptor: this can clinch identification immediately. A gliding eagle (and they often travel long distances in a prolonged, fairly fast glide) can be more difficult to identify, especially when the wings are not fully extended, as is often the case. Then one must assess things like the relative length of tail and the prominence of the head and neck—or keep the bird in view in the hope that it will do something else and show its shape better.

Luckily, eagles frequently glide with their wings almost fully extended, just raised above the level of their backs and with the outer feathers pointing slightly back. In this attitude, the wings appear very long in relation to the body,

6

the ample tail protrudes well to the rear, and the head and neck are quite obvious. This combination of long wings, relatively long tail and obvious head produces an outline quite different from that of the Common Buzzard, which is discussed below. Golden Eagles soar frequently too, with wings fully extended, raised into a very shallow 'V' and often seeming to reach upwards and forwards. The outermost flight-feathers or primaries are fully spread, just like the fingers of a hand. As the birds drift along over a high ridge, or circle slowly in wide sweeps across the sky, often at a great height, we can again appreciate the relative proportions of wings, body and tail referred to above.

With a lot of practice, it is possible to identify eagles even after the briefest glimpse of a distant bird, but problems do arise, even for experienced observers, because the Common Buzzard occurs in eagle country. One sees far more Buzzards than Golden Eagles and they are also large birds of prey, rather similar in outline and flying habits. Optimistic observers often try to make Buzzards into eagles, but it is worth bearing in mind a simple maxim which says that while it is not too difficult to imagine that a Buzzard is an eagle, it is hard to think that an eagle could be anything else. Equally, it is worth bearing in mind that probably every large bird of prey perched on a telegraph pole or similar vantage point close to a road is a Buzzard and not an eagle.

The Common Buzzard is actually much smaller than the Golden Eagle, relatively more compact in build and, when seen soaring or gliding, has a shorter tail, a smaller head and a much less powerful bill. Most Buzzards one sees will be soaring aloft, when their raised and forward-reaching wings, often with the tips distinctly upfurled, and their short, well-spread tails give them a characteristic appearance. Perhaps the best way to appreciate how they differ from eagles is to look at the drawings on page 5. Note how an eagle's wing is relatively longer and narrower towards the tip, 'bulges' at the rear behind the carpal joint and narrows slightly towards the body; note too the different head-shapes and how an eagle's tail is almost as long as its wings are wide. Buzzards are incredibly variable, and some very dark birds, especially at long range, can look almost as uniform in colour as eagles— but most Buzzards show at least some patterning beneath the wings and almost always have dark wing-tips contrasting with paler flight-feathers and dark patches around the bend of the wing. Dark chest and belly markings are also very characteristic of most Buzzards, and the bars on the under-sides of their tails can often be seen quite easily.

WHERE TO SEE THE GOLDEN EAGLE . . . Before describing how one might track down the Golden Eagle, we should put our Scottish birds into perspective in terms of their world distribution. They have a world-wide range in the Northern Hemisphere, and indeed it has been suggested that they could be the most abundant large eagles in the world. In Europe, they occur in virtually all the main mountainous regions, north from Spain and the Mediterranean to Arctic Scandinavia and then eastwards into Russia and Asia; a few small population pockets are known in parts of North Africa and the bird may also occur in Arabia. They are more or less widespread right across central and northern Asia, as far as Japan, but are absent from southern Asia and India. In North America they are found from Alaska southwards, through the Rocky Mountains and adjacent regions as far as Mexico, eastwards across Canada and then southwards again into parts of the eastern United States.

Several centuries ago, the Golden Eagle was found in the Welsh mountains, in the Pennines of England and in Ireland as well as in Scotland. Old records are notoriously imprecise, but we know that eagles ceased to breed in Wales and in their last English outposts in the Lake District before 1800. In Ireland they survived into this century, but the last pair bred in 1912. For most of the twentieth century, then, our national population was confined to Scotland, but here too they vanished from the Southern Uplands after a while and, as breeding birds, were strictly confined to the Highlands. However, since the 1939-45 war, several interesting changes have taken place, beginning with the recolonisation of south-west Scotland. Then a single pair set up home in Northern Ireland, on the Antrim coast, and bred successfully from 1953 to 1960, though unfortunately none has done so since those years. The last decade has seen a return to the Lake District, after an absence of around 200 years, and there are increasing signs of a slow recolonisation of the uplands of north-west England. Eagles also returned to sites in the Hebrides which they had abandoned earlier, and a single pair is now nesting again in Orkney—where none had done so since 1844 or thereabouts.

Today, there are normally three or four pairs (there have been five) in the Southern Uplands, but the bulk of the Scottish population is to be found to the north and west of the Highland Line. Nobody knows precisely how large the population is, but the best estimates we have place it between 250 and 300 breeding pairs. A recent survey of the whole of Britain and Ireland, carried out by the British Trust for Ornithology and the Irish Wildbird Conservancy, plotted the presence or absence of all breeding species on a 10-kilometre grid. From what was found out about Golden Eagles, a figure of at least 236 pairs was given, but this is probably an underestimate. Whatever the true figure, there can be no doubt that there are a lot of eagles in Scotland. We shall return later to the question of how well this population is faring.

Theoretically, one might see a Golden Eagle on most of the larger islands of the Inner and Outer Hebrides (and on a number of the smaller ones too), or anywhere from the Mull of Kintyre northwards through the whole mass of the Highlands into parts of Caithness. The broad crescent of generally low-lying and largely agricultural land which runs from the Firth of Tay up to Aberdeenshire and then round the coast as far as the Dornoch Firth lacks eagles, and they are rare in Caithness. Orkney has but one pair and there is none is Shetland.

Eagles are birds of real Highland country: birds of the wide empty moorlands and wild hillsides and glens which are so much a part of the region. Generally speaking, they tend to avoid the more fertile valley-bottoms of some of the larger glens and straths, as well as well-wooded country—although they may well wander down to the edges of both types of habitat and sometimes nest around the edge of a wood or in an area of scattered trees on a hillside. In areas of the north and west they are found along rocky coasts, and in some of the Western Isles they live near the sea and are hardly mountain birds at all. In many ways, the Golden Eagle seems to have replaced the big White-tailed Eagle or Erne which was so much a part of the coastal scene in the north and west 150 years ago, but was gradually exterminated until the last pair bred during the First World War. In passing, we might mention that attempts are now being made to reintroduce the Erne in the north-west. That is really another story, but if the attempts are successful it will be interesting to see what happens to those pairs of Golden Eagles which now seem to occupy the niche held by the Erne in days gone by.

It is not easy to get precise directions as to where to see an eagle, and certainly those who are 'in the know' are seldom, if ever, willing to disclose the precise whereabouts of nests, or even the particular areas where breeding pairs are most likely to be seen. There is always a good reason for all this secrecy, as we shall see later. Unfortunately, even well-meaning observers can cause a lot of unnecessary disturbance and harassment to nesting pairs, some of which are already subjected to more than their fair share of persecution from other sources.

. . . AND HOW TO FIND IT Personally, I feel that seeking out the Golden Eagle by attempting to visit an eyrie site is the wrong way to go about it. To me, and I believe to many others who enjoy seeing the big birds, there is a greater thrill in watching an eagle soaring above a mountain or methodically quartering a hill slope, even when the bird is far off. Normally, birds away from the nesting area will stay in

Adult Golden Eagle at a typical cliff eyrie

view longer, and there is often the chance of seeing some action and spectacular flying.

Although eagles are widely distributed, they are also rather thinly scattered over huge areas of upland country. The very nature of the terrain they like best, much of which is away from roads, and also the fact that they may spend hours doing nothing, can make them difficult to find, to the casual observer at least. It is possible to spend days driving around in eagle country without seeing one at all—and often Highland weather is a distinct hindrance—but anyone who does a lot of motoring in the Highlands and keeps his eyes open will see eagles from time to time. Usually they are far off, or very high over a ridge or hill slope, and of course there are those frustrating times when the traffic makes it impossible to stop anyway—but every now and then there is the unexpected bonus of a really close view. The first Golden Eagle I ever saw passed within 100 yards of the car on a small road above Balmoral, and once, near Loch Fyne, I came close to hitting one which crossed the road in front of me. On one memorable early spring morning I had marvellous views of a bird hunting almost alongside the main road not far from Carrbridge.

Such chance encounters are all very well, but I have found that systematic searching usually pays better dividends than relying on luck alone. It is well worth spending some time over a drive through mountain country, stopping frequently and carefully scrutinising all the high tops, ridges and slopes within sight—not just once, but several times over. There will be blank days, but then there will be others when you will experience one of the greatest thrills birdwatching has to offer as you suddenly spot a big, black-looking bird sailing along on the skyline, or circling with deceptive slowness around some great crag or rocky outcrop. Binoculars are essential for this sort of thing, of course, and a telescope, if you can use one properly, is even better. Perhaps I can best illustrate how successful these methods can be by harking back to the days when I used to drive fairly regularly from Edinburgh up to Speyside. Sometimes the stretch from somewhere around Calvine up over the Drumochter Pass to Dalwhinnie seemed to take as long as the rest of the journey! I used to stop often and glass all around the higher ground continuously. By doing this I saw single eagles on a number of occasions, and late one afternoon watched two playing together above a big whaleback of a hill. They both landed on the ground several times, and one was even chased off by an irate black-faced sheep which simply put its head down and charged!

The best way to see eagles, though, is to leave the roads altogether and to go onto the hills to find them. This need not entail a vast amount of walking or scrambling, since one can often reach a high vantage-point overlooking a very large expanse of country and then simply sit down to watch and wait. There are certain signs to look out for: grouse or Ptarmigan suddently erupting from the ground and hurtling away at high speed can signal the presence of a hunting eagle, as can agitated behaviour by birds like Curlew and Golden Plover. Ravens and Hooded Crows can be the best allies of all to the eagle-watcher: they will soon spot an eagle if one comes into their bailiwick and then harry and chase it relentlessly, sometimes in small groups, and even when this is going on a great distance away you will be unlucky not to notice it. Once, when I was catching my breath on the stiff climb up from the Mull of Kintyre lighthouse to the car-park far above, I noticed a cloud of tiny specks over the cliffs perhaps a mile and a half away. When I put my glasses on them, they turned out to be a gang of Hoodies and, sure enough, there below was an eagle, gliding fast and twisting this way and that as he sought to shake off his tormentors.

While looking for eagles, it is possible that you will happen on an occupied nest. If you do, please leave it well alone and do not spend too much time near it. The adults may stay away altogether while you remain in the area, and I have known a number of cases where they have deserted eyries because over-eager observers disturbed them too much. They tend to be shy and rather wary birds, so please consider their welfare first.

ANATOMY OF A HUNTER   Having introduced the Golden Eagle and said a little about its distribution and how it might be tracked down, we turn now to look at its way of life in rather more detail. We will consider how it is adapted for its role as a bird of prey, how it hunts and kills, what it eats and how it stands in relation to its prey species.

Apart from its great size and the impression of strength and power it conveys, an eagle shows only too well how it has evolved to live a carnivorous life. It has a large and strongly hooked bill and big feet equipped with strong toes and long, sharp, curved talons. Although the bill may be used to administer the *coup de grâce* to a victim not killed outright, it is not, as many suppose, an offensive weapon but mainly used to tear up prey. It can rip into a carcass very quickly and when a Rabbit, for example is held firmly in the feet, the eagle can dismember it with astonishing efficiency; but the bill can also be used with great delicacy when a female is feeding tiny morsels to a small eaglet. I watched a fully grown young eagle, orphaned and brought up by my friend John Murray, spend a good fifteen minutes picking microscopic pieces of meat from its toes and talons after feeding, and doing so with incredibly delicate movements.

The talons are the eagle's killing apparatus. We shall see how an eagle captures and kills its prey a little later, but for the moment it is enough to say that the immensely powerful feet exert a grip so stong as to kill outright most prey animals. It is not merely the grip which does this, but the way in which it drives the great talons deep into the vital parts of the victim. Again watching the bird mentioned above, I saw for myself just how powerful the grip of an eagle can be. It became excited whenever John came to feed it, and on one occasion when he was manning it in falconry fashion on his arm it gripped him hard enough to bruise his forearm quite badly, even through the stout leather gauntlet he was wearing. I have seen the effect of the talons too. Some years ago, with Douglas Weir, I was in a remote glen where we had gone to investigate a report of an eagle killing lambs. One lamb we looked at had indeed been killed by one of the local birds: one

14

Female eagle at the nest, bringing in a fresh sprig of Rowan

great foot had grasped the lamb across the shoulders and the talon wounds were both large and deep. One talon, probably that on the hind toe, had smashed right through one of the lamb's shoulder-blades. The animal must have been killed instantly.

Seen in close-up, an eagle's 'face' suggests a curious blend of ferocity and nobility. These impressions come mainly from the eye, or rather from the way it is positioned beneath a sort of lowering eyebrow which is in fact a projecting ridge of bone on the skull—the supra-orbital ridge. This is a feature shared by many of the most active killers among the birds of prey, and has a protective function: an eagle's eye is one of the most wonderful of the bird's assets. To be 'eagle-eyed' is to possess exceptionally keen vision, but perhaps we do not realise what this really means until we consider the remarkable eyesight of the bird itself.

An eagle's eye is large in relation to the size of its head. It provides colour vision, probably rather like our own, and because the eyes are placed well to the front of the skull an eagle has binocular vision, again like ours although over a narrower field of view. Binocular vision is very important to a bird which is an active hunter since it enables the bird to locate its prey with great accuracy. It is something we ourselves take for granted—until perhaps we damage an eye and discover just how hard it is to judge distances with only one. Most birds, especially those which are the hunted rather than the hunters, have their eyes positioned on the sides of their head; this gives them varying degrees of all-round vision which is very important to them in their ceaseless watch for approaching danger. An eagle has a certain amount of all-round vision, but like other birds of prey has made some sacrifices in favour of binocular vision to the front.

There is no doubt that an eagle's ability to see small objects and to identify detail at great distances is far superior to ours. Some authorities have suggested that an eagle's visual acuity may be seven or eight times greater than our own. Whatever the arithmetic, a Golden Eagle can undoubtedly locate and identify its prey at incredibly long range and from high altitudes. This remarkable ability comes from the structure of the eye itself. The retina contains specially sensitive visual cells, of which the cones (so called from their shape) deal particularly with visual acuity. Broadly speaking, the greater the number of cones clustered together, the better the perception which can be achieved. In eagles and other birds of prey each retina contains two depressions or foveae, one facing forwards and the other to the side, in which the cones are more numerous than elsewhere and concentrated close together, resulting in a very high degree of visual acuity.

THE MASTER OF ITS ELEMENT Armed with its powerful killing apparatus and equipped with special long-range vision for locating its prey, the Golden Eagle must then be able to move about the huge areas it inhabits with the minimum expenditure of energy. To do this, it has very long, broad wings in relation to its weight and body size—a low wing-loading in aeronautical terms—which are the characteristics of most birds of prey which hunt in open country. Its long wings are designed for long-range operations during which the bird spends much more time gliding than flapping. The large surface area of the wings, in addition to that provided by the ample tail, give the bird considerable 'lift' and enable it to make the maximum use of the air currents which are so much a feature of the terrain it inhabits. Wing flapping is kept to a bare minimum, since this uses up a lot of energy, and is seldom sustained. Gliding is much the most important method of flying, and although the Golden Eagle may lack the special refinements of the real master-gliders, the great albatrosses and their allies (whose wing-shape is similar to that of man's gliders), it is highly proficient and a good deal more versatile.

For all its alertness, an eagle can look an awkward bird at rest and even ungainly while walking about, but once in the air it is transformed and becomes the master of its element. It will fly in rain or snow when it has to, and not even the most ferocious gale will deter an eagle from going about its business. Indeed, I would say that to see a Golden Eagle riding a mountain-top gale is to see the bird at its finest. Perhaps a Peregrine has the edge over a Golden Eagle for sheer speed and manœuvrability (and in the latter aspect I would include the much slower Raven too), but somehow nothing can equal the effortless flying of an eagle gliding along a ridge, side-slipping down a long scree or simply drifting around a deep corrie. When gliding into the wind, using gravity to sustain its forward momentum but maintaining its height through the amount of lift it gets from its wings and tail, the bird can move very fast indeed; it can also operate very slowly, sometimes stopping completely and simply hanging in the sky with hardly any movement from its wings and tail. The bird is usually going much faster than one thinks. I once timed an eagle in a long, slightly downward glide over a measured two miles and was surprised to find that he was travelling at over 60 m.p.h. Other observers have timed the bird at well over 100 m.p.h., and certainly I have seen birds travelling downwind at tremendous pace.

By a simple and often very spectacular process of going into a dive, eagles can descend very rapidly, but they never lose control and show breathtaking precision in pulling out of dives when they drop onto the eyrie or pitch on some favourite outcrop of rock. On one occasion, as I was sitting some way from and slightly above a line of crags where there was an occupied eyrie, I saw the female eagle go past me in a long, fast glide—a sort of flat but very rapid dive. Her intention was to chase off a male Kestrel which was simply flying across the glen from one side to the other. When the little falcon saw her coming, he called in alarm and went into a dive too, downwards and away, seconds before the eagle passed behind him like a thunderbolt. Such was the eagle's speed and size that she needed several hundred yards to come about, but as she did so she swept upwards and increased her altitude advantage over the smaller bird. Kestrels are no mean fliers themselves and can certainly produce a fair turn of speed when pressed, but to my astonishment the eagle

Leaving the eyrie—note the long, broad wings and widely separated flight-feathers

brought off a second and even more spectacular dive and once more passed just behind the falcon before he could make his escape. I doubt if the eagle intended to strike the Kestrel, but whatever her motives, she produced one of the greatest feats of flying I have seen by any bird.

In speaking of eagles in flight one should also mention soaring, when the birds float lazily in wide spirals and not infrequently rise so high that they are lost to the naked eye. Through a pair of 10 × 50 binoculars, I have seen an eagle become a mere speck above me. The birds are not hunting when they do this, although they no doubt spy out the lie of the land and locate likely prey some of the time. The main function of soaring seems to be territorial advertisement, when the male simply shows himself to his nearest neighbours. Soaring also forms part of the display between the members of a pair, and will sometimes precede the spectacular display-flying described later. A pair of eagles will often soar together, and, since they are not normally very aggressive towards other eagles, two pairs may even come together away from the immediate vicinity of their nests. I have often thought that eagles soar purely for enjoyment. This may be an unscientific view, but it is a difficult one to resist!

HUNTING AND KILLING Although the Golden Eagle can be a spectacular and at times extremely rapid flier, it usually hunts and kills in a methodical and unspectacular way. It is not usually the fast-moving, dynamic killer of popular imagination, although eagles can and do kill other birds on the wing from time to time and, more rarely, may strike from a lightning power-dive from a great height. Very early one morning, during the Golden Eagle Survey, I went to look at a site which had not been used for many years but which was unexpectedly occupied again. As I made a quick check of the eyrie (which contained young) I saw the adult eagles in the distance. The male then passed over me several times, and was clearly watching what I was doing. When I

20

left the small side-glen where the eyrie was situated, he followed me, drifting along the ridge high above. A cock Ring Ouzel saw him coming too, and chattered his alarm-call; then the eagle simply turned on one wingtip, closed his wings and dived after the small bird. I had no doubt at all from the speed of the attack that the eagle meant to kill, and because he had descended almost vertically down a couple of hundred yards of the rocky hillside he was overhauling the Ring Ouzel very rapidly as it too dived in a bid to escape. In the last fraction of a second, the Ring Ouzel slipped into a tangle of boulders and went to ground—a lucky escape indeed!

Normally, though, a hunting eagle uses a method common to many other birds of prey which hunt in open country. Patience and thoroughness, plus the possibility of surprise, form the basis of its technique. For something like half an hour one morning, along the Dulnain, from where I could see a wide expanse of hill country, I watched a Golden Eagle hunting. When I first saw the bird it was gliding slowly, close to the ground, steering by small movements of its tail and wingtips with an occasional deep flap of its wings to maintain its forward momentum. It was methodically quartering an open hillside of rough grass and heather, slowly zigzagging across it in the hope of surprising a grouse or perhaps a hare. If it had done so, a brief burst of speed and a quick strike would have ended the chase. Sometimes it slipped down a gully, or around a boulder or two, no doubt hoping to take something unawares. I did not see a kill, but the dogged persistence of the search was most impressive to watch.

After a while, the eagle moved up to a long ridge and varied the original method with some rather faster gliding—again no doubt hoping to take its prey by surprise and perhaps using the extra speed because it was now after Red Grouse, the most likely prey in that habitat. Indeed, I soon saw some grouse get up and rocket away well ahead of the big bird. This was the safest thing for them to do, for unless an eagle has some altitude advantage to increase its acceleration, it has to work hard to fly down a Red Grouse in a level chase.

In fact when an eagle is hunting a grouse-moor the birds often get up and scatter in all directions. I saw one strike, but it was unsuccessful. The eagle surprised a small covey of grouse and plunged in among them, but they evidently saw him just in time and were soon airborne themselves, leaving the eagle to take off again and continue his relentless search along the hilltop.

Hunting, then, can be a prolonged business, and for all the eagle's persistence, agility, speed and strength it may strike unsuccessfully several times before making a kill. This underlines the need for economy of effort while hunting and shows why an ability to glide on and on is so important. It is interesting to reflect that even the most experienced eagle-watchers, after years and years on the hills, see the actual kill only rarely. I have seen a few unsuccessful strikes, but the only kill I witnessed was of a small bird, either a Skylark or a Meadow Pipit, pounced on by an eagle which was fully half a mile away from me at the time.

THE FOOD OF THE GOLDEN EAGLE   Of all the tales about eagles, I suppose those describing what it eats—and in what quantities—are the most unrealistic. The birds are credited with killing full-grown sheep and even Red Deer, while utterly incredible tales persist of them carrying off human babies. There is no truth at all in this last bit of folklore, and I would be very surprised indeed to see an authenticated account of an eagle killing a sheep. Lambs are another matter and we will come back to them later on. Deer fawns may be killed when very small, or if they are sickly. There are records from overseas of Golden Eagles attacking small species of deer, including Roe, but I am not aware of any genuine account from Scotland.

Even so, there are authentic records of some rather unlikely prey species. Friends who are just as sceptical as I am have told me of an adult eagle which killed a full-grown Fox, and of another which killed cock Capercaillies—the turkey-sized gamebirds of the old Scottish pine forests. I also

A male eagle (foreground) arrives at the eyrie with a Rabbit. The larger, bulkier female is behind

know of a small terrier being lifted by an eagle, although it was dropped soon afterwards, and have seen a photograph of a black-and-white cat brought to an eagle's eyrie. No doubt eagles do occasionally kill and carry off such unlikely creatures, but this is rare. The fact is that eagles, like many birds of prey, are opportunist hunters and may kill almost anything within reason should the chance arise. Very small prey is by no means ignored, and if one were to draw up a list of all the creatures recorded in Scotland it would be a very long one indeed. It would include mice, voles, rats, Weasels, Stoats, Red Squirrels, Fox cubs, Wild Cat kittens and even Hedgehogs. The bird list is far longer and includes the small chicks of many ground-nesters and a variety of small birds from the size of Meadow Pipits upwards. Some eagles kill numbers of crows, and some of the coastal pairs exist almost entirely on seabirds such as Manx Shearwaters and Puffins. Whatever the prey, it is mostly taken on or close to the ground, though birds are sometimes captured in mid-air.

Medium-sized mammals seem to be the favourite prey in many parts of Scotland. Rabbits are much to the eagle's liking and individuals may travel a long way to catch them where they are abundant. The Brown Hare is relished too, as is the Blue or Mountain Hare which replaces it at higher altitudes and is generally the commoner of the two in eagle country. Gamebirds make up the other important group of prey species, principally Red Grouse on heather moorland and Ptarmigan on the high tops. Black Grouse may be taken too, and the occasional Capercaillie by some pairs. In summary, we can say that most Scottish eagles prefer hares, Rabbits, Red Grouse and Ptarmigan where these are available, but they also adapt to local conditions and sources of food, as in the case with coastal pairs.

There is one important addition, namely carrion. Yet another misconception concerning the Golden Eagle is that it only eats what it has killed for itself, but, like many other eagles, it will take very readily to carrion, and will in some areas use it as a major source of food. In Scotland, sheep and deer carrion is very important to some eagles, especially in

24

winter when the going is hard, and particularly in the Western Highlands where 'natural' prey is relatively scarce. Dead hill sheep are reasonably numerous, so are their offspring at lambing time, and eagles in sheep country benefit accordingly. Sadly, the eagles' largely innocent scavenging leads people to think they are great killers of sheep and lambs but, as we shall see, this is not the case. A whole deer lying dead on a hillside will feed an eagle for a long time, and the gralloch left during the stalking season will not be overlooked either.

GROUSE AND LAMBS It is as well to look at the Golden Eagle in relation to two particular species it eats, Red Grouse and lambs. These are the subjects of some controversy between the pro- and anti-eagle lobbies and are at the root of the persecution of eagles discussed at the end of this book. At the outset, it is necessary to underline one very important principle which applies to all predatory creatures. This is that the availability of prey controls the numbers and breeding success of the predator; the reverse is not the case. It is the refusal by some people to accept this fundamental law of nature which leads them to persecute predatory species, or to feel that the only good eagle is a dead one. To be perfectly fair, circumstances sometimes arise when birds of prey *can* control the numbers of their prey, but this is usually only a local and temporary phenomenon; it can of course arise where man so alters the natural balance of animal populations as to provide easy pickings for a predator. As far as Scottish Golden Eagles are concerned, however, these reversals are highly unlikely to occur and it is the natural law which applies.

It is probably true to say that most people are totally unconcerned about which wild creatures an eagle kills, and in what numbers, unless these are Red Grouse. The Red Grouse is a famous and much-prized sporting bird, assiduously encouraged and protected on grouse-moors maintained for them. Grouse shooting is a lucrative business, and anything which interferes may find itself at the business end of a gamekeeper's gun. Whether you agree with grouse shooting or not, it cannot be denied that in many parts of the Highlands it is part of a traditional way of life and also a source of employment for many. For these reasons, a great deal of research has been done on the life of the Red Grouse, most notably by the Unit of Grouse and Moorland Ecology at Blackhall, near Banchory. Part of this research has included detailed studies of the birds' predators. It has been shown conclusively that eagles do not adversely affect grouse stocks or 'bags'; indeed, the grouse they kill are part of a surplus produced each year which would die anyway, whether they were shot or not. Like all predators, eagles also tend to kill the easiest prey available and will select the weakest and least fit birds. There are no grounds for persecuting eagles on the basis that they kill too many grouse: the results of the research are there in black and white for all to read but, as we shall see, they are often ignored or glossed over. Another basis for removing eagles is that they will sometimes appear over a grouse moor during a shoot and, by scattering the birds, spoil a day's sport. I will leave the reader to make up his own mind about the ethics of this, but in passing will mention that one or two shooting friends have told me that it is often quite easy to move an eagle on without resorting to shooting at it or paying a visit to its eyrie.

The other problem concerns eagles and sheep—or, more correctly, eagles and lambs, since I doubt if there are any shepherds about nowadays who seriously believe that Golden Eagles kill sheep. In large areas of the Western Highlands and in the Hebrides sheep are all-important and lamb mortality is a constant worry. There is a curious mixture of attitudes over the eagle/lamb problem. It is exceedingly difficult to find anyone who has actually seen an eagle kill a lamb, but not at all hard to find those who assert that it happens all the time and who strongly dislike the birds and label them as inveterate killers of livestock. One does meet plenty of shepherds, however, who are quite happy to have eagles around. Some years ago, on Mull, I was informed by

Adult bringing heather to the nest. One eaglet is in down

one man that he was ready to shoot any eagle which came close enough "because they take my lambs"—though he was very evasive when I asked him how many and how often. The shepherd on the next holding held the opposite view and "liked to see the eagle about the place". He was evasive too—about precisely where the local pair were nesting that year!

So what is the truth? It is not completely straightforward, but there is no doubt that most claims of eagles slaughtering lambs are either wholly unfounded or grossly exaggerated. Some protectionists who have claimed that eagles never kill lambs have, I hope, changed their views by now: a few eagles certainly do so, but normally only in very small numbers and hardly ever, it seems, on a regular basis. The majority of lambs eaten by eagles or taken up to eyries have been picked up as carrion. Only one serious study of the problem has been published so far, and this was carried out on Lewis by Jim Lockie and David Stephen, both well-known authorities on Highland wildlife who, despite the regard I know they both have for the Golden Eagle, were quite prepared to come out against the birds if the case against them were proven. They carried out a critical inquiry to see if local claims that eagles were killing large numbers of lambs were justified. In the event, they were able to exonerate the eagles completely and pointed instead to poor land and livestock management as the root causes of the undoubtedly heavy mortality among young lambs. From my own conversations with shepherds and fellow eagle-men, I hold the view that a broadly similar situation applies in most, if not all, other sheep areas in the west.

A problem remains, however. An eagle which kills a small number of lambs may get away with it where there is a large stock of sheep on the hill, or may even be tolerated for misdeeds which, after all, are confined to a short period when the lambs are immature. But a crofter with a small flock could have a real problem: if he rears only a few lambs each year, an eagle which reduces his final total by even one or two animals is more than just a nuisance. I was marginally involved in one such case some years ago with my friends Douglas Weir and Lea MacNally. An eagle was clearly killing lambs and there was evidence of this on and around the eyrie. I think we were all a little upset to realise that the solution would be to remove one or possibly both of the adult eagles. We were very relieved when an alternative solution offered itself and, under licence, the young bird in the eyrie was taken and given to Edinburgh Zoo, which happened to require a Golden Eagle at that time. It was eventually put on show at the zoo and became a firm favourite with visitors. I often wondered what they would have said had they been aware of how it came to be there!

In a few areas, a case might be made out for control measures against a few eagles. I would add, however, that I believe strongly that no action should be taken until every case has been fully investigated. I am opposed to people taking the law into their own hands, especially as this is often done on the flimsiest evidence or simply as the result of a strong prejudice against eagles. It would be possible to provide compensation if this is really necessary—but I have grave reservations about this too. It would be all too easy to abuse the system at the expense of the Golden Eagle, as well as of the taxpayer.

What is needed is a long-term investigation into the eagle/lamb controversy, particularly in parts of the Outer Hebrides where the eagle often seems to be nobody's friend. Much more evidence is required before any decision is taken to change the present situation whereby the Golden Eagle is fully protected by law. A start was made in fact in the Uists in 1976, by the Nature Conservancy Council. One hopes that this will lead on to a much fuller study over a wider area in the years ahead.

On the basis of what it eats and what effects it has on its prey, the Scottish eagle only rarely conflicts with man's interests and, if one is to be honest, has a negligible impact on either his livestock or his sporting activities. It might be hard to make out a case for the eagle as a 'beneficial bird'—but all the evidence we have shows quite clearly that to regard it as 'vermin' is utter nonsense. On balance, in material terms at any rate, it is probably best regarded as 'neutral'.

HOW MUCH IS KILLED? Nobody who has ever handled a Golden Eagle can doubt that it is an enormously strong bird and, as we have seen, it can kill prey as large as itself and considerably heavier. In Scotland the largest and heaviest item taken commonly is a full-grown Brown Hare, which may weigh up to 9 lb. On most occasions, such a large creature will prove too heavy for the bird to carry away whole and will be dismembered and removed bit by bit. Eagles cannot normally carry the equivalent of their own weight, and indeed some recent experiments carried out in the United States, using a captive bird released from a tower, have shown that even a weight of 2½ lb attached to its legs greatly hindered its flying ability. Nevertheless, how much an eagle can carry will depend to some extent on wind conditions, and in some of the incredibly strong winds which arise in mountain country there seems little doubt that an eagle can lift off with a full-grown hare, or perhaps something even bigger, and carry it for at least a short distance. I have seen a lamb brought to a slope below an eyrie and estimated that it weighed around 10 lb, but it seemed that the bird was quite unable to lift it further.

Three important questions remain to be answered: how much food does a Golden Eagle require to lead an active and healthy life; do eagle numbers depend on how much food is available to them; and does the amount of prey they can find govern their breeding success, as it seems to do with some other birds of prey in Britain?

Studies carried out on captive eagles show that an adult needs 8-10 oz of food per day to survive. It is thought that similar figures apply for wild birds, but no accurate data exists at present—and would, in any case, be rather difficult to obtain. When the opportunity arises, eagles will eat perhaps six or seven times this average amount, literally gorging themselves; afterwards, they are well able to go for

While the chicks are small, they are carefully tended and fed by the hen eagle

several days at a time without feeding. This ability is beneficial to a bird which may not be able to feed, or even hunt, every day in winter. Exactly how long a wild eagle might be able to go without food has never been established, but it is a fair assumption to say that it will experience no real hardship if it has to fast for a week or so. Captive birds have been known to survive quite happily without eating at all for as long as three weeks.

Taking into account the prey an eagle tackles, large and small, a certain proportion is not eaten and, in addition, the bird does not digest all that it swallows: like other birds of prey, it forms 'pellets' of indigestible matter (bones, teeth, fur and so on) which are later ejected via the mouth. The portion of prey which is not eaten is known as the 'waste factor', and it has been calculated that this is of the order of 20 to 30 per cent by weight of all live kills. Bearing this in mind, an adult eagle must kill roughly 235 lb of prey species in a year, of which it will digest about 175 lb. But in practice many eagles probably do not reach these figues since, to a greater or lesser extent, part of their food requirement is made up of carrion.

The classic food study of Scottish eagles was carried out in the early 1960s by two of our most eminent eagle experts, Adam Watson and Leslie Brown. For the purposes of their study, they divided Highland eagle country into four main zones, basing these on the nature of the terrain and the density of potential prey available in them. We need not go into detail here, but broadly speaking the Eastern Highlands are richer in food from an eagle's point of view than the Western Highlands and the north-west. To provide a baseline, they calculated that an average pair of eagles in their 'home range' (a term discussed later, but essentially meaning the total area in which a pair of eagles nest and hunt), plus their young of the year and any sub-adult or unattached eagles living in the same area, would together require about 620 lb of food in any one year. Taking into account the waste factor, the actual amount eaten would be about 550 lb. Of this, they suggested that, on average, 110 lb would be carrion, 280 lb would be mammals and 160 lb would be birds. Looked at in terms of actual animals and birds, these figures could represent, say, seventy Mountain Hares and 126 Red Grouse. Since the availability of carrion, mammals and birds varies from zone to zone, some variation in these figures would obviously occur at a local level. For instance, in sheep country in the Western Highlands the carrion figure would be higher, and the figure for grouse much lower. Since one often hears that eagles kill, for example, enormous numbers of grouse, it is worth bearing these figures in mind. I have been assured by gamekeepers that a pair of eagles kill twenty to thirty grouse per week on their beats—or 1,000-1,500 birds per year—which is quite ridiculous when set against the birds' known food requirements. Even if two pairs hunt a single area, these totals would never be reached. If such wildly exaggerated stories were true, it would mean the eagles kill vastly more prey then they could ever eat, which simply does not happen. It is another of nature's basic laws that any predator will normally only kill what it requires to eat and to feed to its offspring—killing for fun or in a random way is most unusual.

One might assume that the size of an eagle's home range would be determined by the amount of food available in it, either as live prey or carrion, or both, but one of the most interesting discoveries made by Brown and Watson was that this is not so. While the smallest home range certainly occurred in the zone richest in potential prey and the largest was in the poorest zone, another almost equally poor zone included home ranges as small as those in the best area. Some workers had also suggested that in the sheep-rich Western Isles eagles had very small home ranges because so much carrion was available for them, but this idea fell down too since the birds were known to range over areas every bit as large as they did elsewhere. It is clear, in fact, that an eagle's home range supports considerable more potential prey than the birds require, and that carrion is no more a controlling factor than is live prey. Realising this, one is bound to ask, 'What is the controlling factor?' The simple answer is that we do not know. One theory is that the birds do not tolerate one another and are strictly and aggressively territorial over very large areas. As we shall see, this is not the case. Another idea is that the availability of nesting sites could be the answer. But neither is this supported by the evidence we have.

33

Generally speaking, it has always been assumed that eagles in the east rear slightly more young per pair per year than those in the west, and that broods of two young surviving to leave the nest are commoner in the east. These assumptions relate to a much richer supply of prey in, say, Deeside than south-west Argyll; indeed, the amount of food available could be five to eight times greater in the east than in the west. A lot of work has been done during the last twenty years on sample populations in various parts of Scotland, and certainly some of the results tend to support both assumptions, although the differences between productivity in the east and west are not proportional to the differences in food availability. Equally, there are some results which hardly support these theories at all, so the picture remains somewhat confused. This is made worse by the fact that, in some areas, the figures for breeding success are affected by external factors—deliberate persecution and other forms of human disturbance. Ideally, the whole question of relating breeding success to food supply could only be answered by complete and very detailed comparative studies of eagles breeding in areas of good and poor food supply but totally undisturbed by man. I think most eagle workers would expect the studies to show the two assumptions made earlier to be valid. Unfortunately, problems of disturbance in some of the food-rich areas in the Eastern Highlands are now becoming so great that there would be considerable difficulty in finding enough unharassed pairs to make up a reasonable sample.

RELATIONS WITH OTHER BIRDS AND ANIMALS In the previous sections, we have considered the relationships between the Golden Eagle and those of its neighbours which it eats. Obviously, eagles do not spend their whole lives hunting, so what happens when they encounter other creatures at other times? Normally, they tend to ignore prey species and most other animals and birds too when not hunting, but exceptions do occur, especially in

The larger first-born chick (left) frequently attacks and kills its younger brother or sister

the immediate area of an occupied eyrie. An eagle may 'buzz' another bird of prey, large or small, and may see off Ravens too; an incident involving a passing Kestrel has already been described.

The most interesting incident I have seen involved a hill Fox which appeared on a long slope of boulders and scree at the head of a valley where I was watching a pair of eagles. The big female eagle, who was on the nest with her single youngster, spotted the Fox long before I did and at once took off and went down towards it in a long, fairly rapid glide. She swooped at it quite deliberately and, swinging upwards, came in for a second, shorter dive. On both occasions she passed within a few feet of the Fox, which flattened its body and tail to the ground each time and bared its teeth in defiance as the eagle swept past. The bird repeated the manœuvre a third time and then, to my surprise, landed on a rock only a few yards from the Fox. Quite suddenly, I caught sight of a dark shape coming fast towards the action—the male eagle, which had been sitting high on the other side of the valley, had come to join in. With perfect precision, he aimed his long, high-speed dive for a spot a few feet from his mate and pitched alongside her. At that point the Fox, no doubt feeling discretion to be the better part of valour, ran quickly to earth among a mass of boulders near by and did not reappear. In due course, the two eagles lost interest and flew off.

Eagles are normally rather wary of man, especially at the nest. A bird will slip away, often quite unobtrusively, as the eyrie is approached, sometimes when an observer is still a mile away—although individual birds vary a great deal in their reactions and incubating females will often sit tight. It also seems that eagles soon come to recognise familiar people—the shepherd or stalker, say, who passes by quite frequently and who may not be associated with danger; a stranger, or someone behaving in an unfamiliar way, might put a bird off much sooner than a regular passer-by. When making quick visits to eyries to check their contents during eagle-survey work, I have sometimes had a feeling of 'being watched' and have looked up just in time to see the familiar dark shape disappearing over the skyline. On several occasions eagles have soared high overhead, obviously watching my every move, while on others they have observed more subtly, appearing briefly above a ridge some way off and reappearing elsewhere a little later. They seldom come very close, and the rarest thing of all is for an eagle to attack a man, and indeed I know of only one authenticated instance of this happening in Scotland.

Eyries will be deserted by incubating birds if they are disturbed suddenly—for example, by a man appearing above the nest—so it was an unwritten rule among eagle-survey workers to make sure the bird saw us coming. I once went up to a small crag with a colleague and, after a while, we located which of the several eyries seemed to be in use that year. While I sat some way off, keeping watch, my companion scrambled up to the nest. The female eagle must have had us in view all the while, although we could not see her from below. As my friend reached the eyrie she stood up and, in that wonderfully unhurried way eagles have, simply walked to the edge of the nest and launched herself into space.

One might imagine that an eagle, which has no real natural enemies other than man, would be left well alone in its domain—a bird to be respected at all times, especially while hunting. But this is not the case. Birds of prey, like some other large birds and animals such as Stoats, Foxes and cats, are subjected to 'mobbing' by their neighbours, which may not necessarily be potential prey: small birds of prey may mob larger ones, for example. This ritualised behaviour has an important survival function. It seldom takes the form of sustained attack (although this does occur), but usually serves to draw attention to a passing predator, with as much noise and agitation as possible, so warning other creatures of approaching danger and persuading the predator to go elsewhere. The pattern of mobbing behaviour, and the predator's reaction to it, is illustrated well in the case of the Golden Eagle.

A perched eagle may not attract much attention, although

it may be subjected to a certain amount of abuse by Meadow Pipits, Ring Ouzels and other small hill birds; crows too may be a nuisance, so much so that an eagle may decide to move on, but I have watched eagles sitting on rocks for long periods during which they were largely ignored by small birds. A flying eagle is another matter: small birds may give chase, though usually not for long, as may birds like Curlews as the eagle passes over their territory. Crows and Ravens, however, often pursue eagerly and persistently with what seems like suicidal enthusiasm; but many eagles simply out-fly these nuisances, with a deft sideslip and a sudden change of direction. Any sort of retaliation is unusual. Sometimes, though, the pace hots up and the smaller birds become ever bolder and more determined, and it is then that the observer may see all sorts of aerobatics as the pursuers press home their attacks and the eagle is forced to take evasive action. He may even roll on his back and present his talons when a crow or Raven ventures really close, and much the same sort of thing occasionally happens in the rather more gentlemanly bouts between eagles and Buzzards.

If a bit of speed or manœuvrability is called for, most eagles seem to be capable of outflying their pursuers without extending themselves, and some have a marvellously disdainful way of floating along, surrounded by diving and gyrating birds and totally ignoring them. I once saw an eagle go into a half-roll, close its wings and pull off a stupendous, near-vertical dive which left all the hangers-on hundreds of feet behind, but such extreme action is usually unnecessary.

There are a few birds, though, which can give an eagle a hard time. A pair of Ravens, themselves fairly fast movers and no mean performers when it comes to manœuvrability, can put an eagle through its paces and cause it to hurry, but in this respect the arch-demon is the Peregrine, a compact, robustly built and exceedingly fast falcon which will harry a passing eagle mercilessly. To see an eagle being mobbed by a Peregrine is an unforgettable experience. Even when an eagle pulls out all the stops it seldom seems to get the better of the smaller bird.

By the time an eaglet is seven weeks old, the feathers on its back and wings are developing rapidly

THE HOME RANGE   So much for eagles and other birds and animals—but what happens when eagles meet one another? Often, the answer is very little. There may be some idle sparring as birds soar together, but normally they are fairly tolerant of one another. The Golden Eagle is not strictly territorial in the sense that a Robin is: it does not actively defend against all other eagles the area in which it lives. It may drive off another eagle which ventures too near its nesting area, but will tolerate other birds in the areas where it hunts. Indeed, the hunting grounds of different pairs of eagles may overlap to some extent without causing friction, or may be shared with an immature bird or perhaps an unmated adult. It is therefore incorrect to describe an eagle's area of operations as its 'territory'; the expression 'home range' is preferable. As we have seen, the size of the home range, which in Scotland is usually 11-13,000 acres, but can be as large as 18,000 acres, does not seem to be limited by the amount of prey it contains, nor by any strictly territorial instincts on the part of the eagles living there. In some areas it is possible that the availability of suitable nest-sites is a limiting factor, but this is certainly not the case in others. On the whole, we are unable to draw any firm conclusions.

PAIRING AND COURTSHIP From what we have learned of the Golden Eagle so far, it can be concluded that in theory at least Scotland is an ideal home for a large population, with no shortage of suitable habitat and an abundance of food. Given that these factors are in the bird's favour, we must now turn to the reproductive cycle, not only to see how eagles set up home and rear their young, but also to discuss whether or not they are faring well in doing so. Are enough young being reared each year, and do enough of them survive to keep the population going? These are vital questions.

In Scotland, adult Golden Eagles are sedentary birds, probably remaining inside their home ranges from the time they are old enough to breed, at four or five years of age, until they die. They pair for life and spend much of their time close to one another, sometimes hunting and foraging together in winter. When one of the pair dies, there are no unhappy widowers or widows left to pine a deceased mate; the missing partner is replaced very quickly by another eagle, which may be an adult of breeding age or even an immature bird. If the latter is the case, the new pair may spend one or two seasons together going through the preliminaries of breeding, but not rearing any young until the newcomer is sexually mature. In a few cases, pairs of immatures may take over vacant home ranges and remain in occupation until they are old enough to breed. Details recently came to light of a pair actually rearing young while one of them was still in sub-adult plumage, so possibly some eagles are sexually mature before they outwardly resemble adults.

The nesting area is the focal point of the year's activity. This is obvious enough during the breeding season, when both adults remain close to or within sight of their eyrie except when away hunting, but even in winter a pair of eagles may be found close to their traditional nest-site. An eyrie site, or some favourite perch close by, is often used as a roost.

Eagles are usually silent birds, not calling very often and even then only producing a rather high bark or a yelping note, or perhaps a short series of such calls. Most eagle watchers will tell you that they have hardly ever heard a Golden Eagle give tongue, but continuous observations at the well-protected nest of the first Lake District pair suggest that adults may in fact communicate by call more often than is generally supposed. At any rate, a male eagle has no song and must therefore advertise his presence by purely visual means. To do this, he will soar for long periods over his home range, especially over the nesting area, often in company with his mate. As they fly together they may indulge in nuptial play high above the home range. Short, playful chases may follow, sometimes with aerobatics, with the female rolling over onto her back to touch talons with the male as he flies close above her.

The male's main display, however, performed throughout the year but often best seen as winter ends and there are fine, clear days above the hills, is one of the most thrilling sights imaginable. To me it conjures up the real essence of the Highlands. Sometimes the cock will go through his paces while the hen is flying with him, but more often he performs alone, or when she is perched somewhere far below, perhaps on the eyrie itself.

One minute he is soaring or gliding along, the next he has folded his wings completely and is dropping earthwards like a stone, coming down through hundreds of feet of air in a steep dive. It is almost impossible to see precisely how he achieves his next manœuvre, but suddenly he is swinging upwards again, still with his wings closed, 'shooting' back to something like his original height. As he loses his upward momentum and seems about to stall, he simply tips forward again and falls away in another dive. This performance is repeated again and again in steep undulations across large expanses of sky. Measuring from a map, I estimated that a male eagle I saw displaying near Dalwhinnie had crossed a mile and a half of sky in this way. Although the display is most marked during late winter and early spring, it goes on to a lesser extent—and sometimes less spectacularly— throughout the nesting season and in other months too. It clearly serves not only as a stimulus to mating but also as a means of maintaining the pair-bond between the eagles throughout their lives together. In some circumstances, an eagle will use this form of display for other reasons. One may see it used if another eagle comes towards the nesting area, and there seems no doubt that it is also used to advertise a bird's presence to his nearest neighbour, who may be only two or three miles away. Females perform very similar displays, but much less often than males, it seems, and often at lower altitudes.

THE EYRIE SITE Golden Eagles are very conservative birds, remaining faithful to traditional nesting sites, some of which have undoubtedly been in use for centuries. It is not all that uncommon for a nest to be used in successive years, but many pairs have at least one alternate site and others have several; some birds may have as many as eight or more. These sites may be either very close together, only feet apart

Eight weeks old—well feathered and well fed

in some cases, or distant from one another—perhaps on different sides of the same glen, or at opposite ends of a long rocky hillside. They may all be rock sites, or all tree sites, or a mixture of the two, and are used in a rough sort of rotation.

Most Scottish eyries are on cliffs or crags, with no particularly favoured direction in which they face, and are anywhere between fifty and 3,000 feet above sea-level, with the highest ones in the Eastern Highlands and the lowest in the west, on sea cliffs, where some are certainly below the fifty-foot contour. A few are easily accessible, and others moderately so, but many more are very difficult to get to and cannot be reached without using skilled mountaineering techniques. I know of one sea-cliff site which cannot be seen at all from the land and is almost invisible from a boat too. All sorts of variations occur with rock sites—some are in the gorge of a burn, or even in a small gully where one would never think of looking, and others are on insignificant outcrops of rock. A very few pairs even nest on the ground in sheltered spots, and one pre-war site I was shown in Sutherland was in rough, open grassland where one might have driven right into it in a reasonably robust vehicle. Some cliff sites may be adjacent to or even partly built onto a small tree such as a Rowan, and may be shaded or partly concealed in this way. Some eyries are incredibly obvious, and there are others which, even to the practised eye, are very hard to spot. The size of the nest will depend on the amount of material available locally, the largest being where the birds can obtain the best supply of sticks and branches to form the main structure. Most are usually only two or perhaps three feet in depth, but are around five or six feet in diameter.

A few pairs have regular tree sites, and indeed some birds never nest anywhere else. Tree eyries are the largest of all, since the nest material tends to accumulate year after year and the nest becomes progressively more massive: a famous one has reached a depth of at least seventeen feet, and a nest I climbed to in a small and ancient Scots Pine was so big—about four feet deep and eight across—that I was unable to see into it. Old pines, especially the rather squat types on lower mountainsides, are the favourites among tree-nesting eagles, but other trees in use include oaks and Rowans. Artificial plantations are usually avoided, but the late Seton Gordon, the doyen of Scottish eagle men, refers to a nest in a larch, and I have seen one in a very small tree near the edge of a block of young pines.

Nest-building may occur at any time of the year, but is most intense between February and March. More than one nest may be built up before breeding begins, with branches and heather stems forming the main base material. The largest branches are carried in the feet, but other items are often brought in the bill. Both birds collect and bring in nest material, but the female probably does the bulk of the building. Green vegetation is added as a lining, with woodrush being a particular favourite, and from the amount brought in

44

one can usually discover which of a series of nests will be used before any eggs are laid.

Fresh vegetation is brought to the nest during the first half of the nesting cycle, but only intermittently after that. An adult arriving at the eyrie often brings in a green sprig of some sort. This is probably ritual behaviour, although sometimes the sprig will be built into the fabric of the nest. It has been suggested that the habit has to do with nest sanitation, covering up the prey remains which soon litter an active nest, but if so it is probably accidental rather than deliberate. I once saw a female eagle collecting extra nest material. She flew from the nest to a small Rowan a few hundred yards away and landed heavily and very clumsily in its crown. After some considerable effort, during which leaves and small twigs were scattered in all directions, she emerged with a small branch, complete with leaves, and brought it up to the nest, flapping laboriously as she carried the unwieldy load in her bill. She then spent a good ten minutes working it into the nest structure before she was satisfied with her efforts.

EGGS AND THE HATCH   March is the month for egg-laying, usually around mid-month or soon afterwards, but even during the first week on rare occasions. An incubating eagle may thus be covering eggs in really bad weather—it is not at all uncommon for birds to be sitting while they are surrounded by snow. The normal clutch size is two eggs, the second laid between three and four days after the first. Some females lay one fertile and one infertile egg, while some others only ever lay one egg; three eggs are occasionally produced, but a clutch of four is exceptionally rare. A Golden Eagle's egg is roughly the size of a goose's egg, off-white in colour but usually spotted or blotched with a varying amount of brown or red-brown, especially near the larger end. In a clutch of two, one egg is often more boldly marked than the other, and virtually unmarked eggs are often laid. In Canada, sixteen eggs laid by a captive eagle between 1964 and 1971 were examined critically while still fresh, using laboratory techniques, and it was concluded that the markings on them were not caused by the normal process of pigmentation but were in effect bloodstains as a result of the rupture of tiny blood vessels during laying. As far as I know, this work has not been followed up elsewhere and I am surprised that it seems to have received very little publicity.

Incubation begins with the laying of the first egg and in Scotland lasts for forty-three to forty-five days. The female often incubates alone, but males may take a share too, at least for short spells when they relieve the female; but even with these pairs it is the female who does the bulk of the 'sitting'. She will sit particularly closely as the time for the hatch approaches, being most reluctant to leave her eggs even when approached by man. Although females have been seen to leave their eggs and make a kill near the nest, this is not normal behaviour and most females probably only leave the nest for short spells to feed on prey brought to some nearby spot by the male. They are rarely, if ever, actually fed by the male on the nest. It appears that the female's need for food is considerably reduced during incubation, as is the case with other eagles.

The difference in timing between the laying of the eggs results in asynchronous hatching—the first eaglet being three or four days old when the second is born. Thus the first-comer is bigger and stronger than its little brother or sister (there is no proof that more females than males are 'first', as has been supposed) and is able to dominate when food is brought to the nest. It will therefore get the first and best pickings and is the more likely to survive. During the first week that the two are together in the nest, a strange phenomenon occurs, one which is ignored by the female, who is usually in close attendance at this stage. The older chick will repeatedly attack and bully the younger and, in roughly eight cases out of ten, actually kills it. If the younger chick contrives to survive until it is about three weeks old, the danger passes. Just why this regular fratricide should occur remains a mystery (it is known in other eagle species

A fully grown young eagle, thirteen weeks old, out of the nest and idly stretching a leg

too). Competition for food or even food availability is not the answer. Even though there is a slight tendency towards pairs in areas of relatively poor food supply rearing fewer young than those from better prey regions, some pairs in the poorer areas rear two young regularly, and there always seems to be enough food to go round at the eyrie. Obviously a good deal of further study is called for, but I suspect that what has been called the 'Cain and Abel' battle between young eagles will continue to puzzle us for many years. In passing, it is worth mentioning that removing the younger chick before it perishes, rearing it in captivity and then releasing it back to the wild will not necessarily 'improve' the eagle population. Whatever prompts this curious form of fratricide clearly has a natural origin, and even if one out of the two young dies in 80 per cent of all eyries it seems clear that it does not affect the intake of new recruits into the population.

THE YOUNG GROW UP   For the first three weeks or so of their lives, the chicks are closely attended by the female eagle, who spends much time on the nest with them and never wanders far away. At this time the male, whose job it is to provide for the whole family, must step up his hunting activities. Often he stays at the nest for only a few seconds after delivering prey, but he will remain longer if the female goes off to feed. When it comes to guarding or brooding the young, however, his is a minor role. While the eaglets are still tiny, their mother tends and feeds them with extraordinary care.

The eaglets are in the nest for ten to eleven weeks in all. They begin life in a first coat of white down, soon to be replaced by a thicker second layer. Their weight increases enormously, and by the time they are between five and six weeks old, they will weigh upwards of thirty times as much as they did at birth. Then comes the period when the production of the first coat of feathers is at its peak and the weight-gains slacken off. About three weeks after hatching, the eaglets are left alone in the nest, though the female is still close at hand and returns from time to time—especially to cover them in bad weather. After six weeks, she leaves them for longer spells, for they are passing out of the stage when she needs to assist them with feeding. During the last few weeks, before the young fly, she joins the male in hunting and bringing food to the nest. By then neither adult spends much time at the eyrie. The young are growing really large, exercising their legs and flapping their wings vigorously. On big ledges they will wander out of the eyrie, but they soon come back when they spot an adult arriving with food. Indeed, from an early age they take a great interest in the comings and goings of their parents and spot them at long distances, calling in their excitement with the weak, querulous cheeping which is the most typical sound at an occupied eyrie. They still call in this way when they are ready to fly, and the cheeps sound quite incongruous coming from such a big bird.

Somewhere around their eleventh week of life, the young make their first flights, often when the parents are away, and certainly with no assistance or coaxing from them. Their first, short flights are often clumsy, but within two or three weeks they are flying strongly. All this time they remain reasonably near the eyrie, often returning to it; but wherever they are their parents find them and continue to bring them food. From egg-laying to fledging, which is normally in early July, takes up to 125 days, so eagles are occupied with breeding matters for a substantial part of the year. Breeding is a prolonged process, then, and if interrupted will be abandoned for the year; there are no records of eagles re-laying if they lose their clutch of eggs.

Before moving on to talk about breeding success and what this means to the Scottish population of eagles, we should attempt to clear up one outstanding point of eagle physiology, namely the difference in size between the male and the female. Eagles are by no means unique in this respect; in most birds of prey, and also in owls, the female is generally larger than the male, the difference being most pronounced in the most active hunters of live prey. Various explanations

49

have been put forward to account for this. One is that a size differential enables a pair of eagles to avail themselves of as wide a range of prey as possible, with the female being able to cope with larger and heavier items—but there is little evidence that she consistently does so. Following this line of reasoning, it is also said that there is some advantage in the female being able to bring in larger prey items at the stage when she joins the male in hunting for the family—that is, at a time when their food requirements are greatest. Again, there is no firm evidence to show that this is the case. There is probably a grain of truth in both these theories, but current opinion favours a more subtle reason for the size difference. It is thought that a fierce and strongly predatory bird may even regard its mate as a possible source of food and that the often complex rituals of behaviour by which birds appease one another and so pair and mate could increase the dominance of the male, who takes the more 'aggressive' role in these matters anyway. To counterbalance this, the female is larger and more powerful and in a sense is able to overawe her mate sufficiently for equilibrium to be achieved.

BREEDING SUCCESS AND SURVIVAL If we are to know whether the Scottish eagle population is increasing, declining or merely holding its own, we must be able to measure breeding success. This means knowing which nests are successful and which fail, and how many young are added to the population. Once we have such figures, we can set them against what we believe to be the norms for a thriving population.

A few long-term studies of eagles in certain areas have been carried out, and these, together with the published results of a five-year period of the Royal Society for the Protection of Birds' continuing Golden Eagle Survey, are the sources of the figures quoted below. Although the figures for the second five-year period of the survey still await publication, they are broadly similar to those we shall be quoting.

From the data available, we can calculate that eagles which are completely free from persecution and nesting failures can rear young at an average rate of 0·8 young per pair per annum. This means potential breeding pairs and takes into account non-breeding years. In any one year, it seems that between 10 and 25 per cent of eagles established in home ranges do not breed—a phenomenon whose causes are unknown but which is common to a number of other large birds of prey. It assumes, then, that the average pair will rear eight young in ten years. It has also been assumed that about 75 per cent of the young die before they are old enough to breed (in their fifth year), so that from the original figure of 0·8 only 25 per cent, or 0·2, survive to reach maturity. Breeding at this rate, a pair of eagles will, over ten years, produce only two young which survive to join the breeding population or, in effect, replace their parents. If we assume that an eagle's breeding life is only as long as the bird takes to replace itself—that is, ten years—and add to that the four or five years the bird spends as an immature, we can estimate that a wild bird will live to an age of fourteen or fifteen.

Three things arise which put in question the validity of these basic statistics. In Scotland, as we shall see, a lot of eagles do not enjoy a life free from persecution and disturbance. This means that in some regions the magic figure of 0·8 is not achieved. Secondly, we have very little information on what happens to young Scottish eagles between the time they leave their parents and their 'coming of age'. Although 75 per cent may be a reasonable mortality estimate based on what we know of other birds of prey, it may not be very accurate for the Golden Eagle. We do know that a young eagle may leave its parents at any time from the October to the winter of its first year—and that, contrary to popular belief, it is not driven off by its parents but goes of its own accord. It seems that it usually leaves its parents' home range, going off to marginal eagle country and perhaps avoiding competition with adults—but what it does next is obscure. One may encounter immature eagles on areas of ground where adults are scarcely ever seen at almost any

51

time—but equally they may turn up in occupied home ranges too and not be molested. On a single day on Mull, at a time when eagles were on eggs, I encountered immatures in the heart of two areas occupied by breeding pairs—one of the young birds within a few hundred yards of an active eyrie. So possibly the biggest question of all concerns the life and survival of young Scottish eagles. A detailed long-term study would be immensely difficult in practical terms, but would undoubtedly produce a lot of the information we lack at the moment.

The third anomaly arises from the actual figures we have for breeding success over the last decade or so, for they show some interesting differences from those quoted so far. The figures quoted here are from the 1964-68 period of the R.S.P.B. survey. Totalling up over the five-year period, we looked at 316 occupied home ranges, or an average of sixty-three per annum (about 20-25 per cent of the entire population), spread over seven sample areas. There were 242 breeding attempts of which 126 ended successfully, with the results unknown in a further thirty-four cases. There were eighty-two known failures. With 142 young reared, the success rate, ignoring the 'results unknown' category, was nearly 0·45 per occupied home range—quite a bit lower than the 0·8 figure quoted earlier. There was a slightly better rate of young per pair in the areas of good food supply as opposed to where it was poor, and the rate varied considerably from area to area owing to different amounts of disturbance and persecution—a point we shall return to later.

Outside the sample areas, miscellaneous results were obtained for the same period for a further 173 occupied home ranges. Breeding took place in 153 of these, with thirty-six known failures, seventy-one known successes and forty-six 'results unknown'. Again ignoring this last category, the production figure was 0·7 per home range. Adding together all the figures, survey and miscellaneous, we score as follows: 489 occupied home ranges, breeding in 395, 118 failures, 197 successes and 80 unknown results. At least 231 young were reared and, still leaving out the 'results unknown', we arrive at an overall figure of 0·56 young per home range per annum. So the grand total likewise falls short of the figure of 0·8.

The odd thing is that the work done on Scottish eagles during the last decade or so seems to show that the population is very nearly stable at this lower figure, or is declining only very slowly. If this is so, and 0·56 is a high enough yearly production rate per occupied home range, then either a pair of eagles have a longer breeding life than stated earlier (about fourteen years instead of ten) or the mortality among immatures is a good bit lower than 75 per cent. Only continuing survey work will solve these mysteries.

PERSECUTION AND DISTURBANCE It is clear from the figures I have quoted that a large number of eagles failed in their nesting attempts between 1964 and 1968—118 out of 315, or 37 per cent. Only a few of these were the result of natural causes: there were cases of eggs failing to hatch and of a few young dying—in both cases for unknown reasons—and I recall one instance of a big, top-heavy nest collapsing and being deserted. Natural failures are obviously rare among Scottish eagles, and certainly all the work done on the birds so far indicates that predation is almost non-existent. It is a sad fact that nearly all the failures can be laid at the door of man—the Golden Eagle's only real enemy. Deliberate persecution took a heavy toll—but so did accidental disturbance.

There is a curious conflict of opinion over eagles in the Highlands and islands. While an increasing number of landowners, keepers, stalkers and shepherds are prepared to tolerate the birds (many of them taking an active interest in their welfare), a large number hold an entirely different view. Some of their attitudes recall those of last century when all birds of prey and owls were classed as 'vermin', because of the damage they were alleged to do to sporting interests particularly, and were slaughtered indiscriminately and in incredible numbers. It is disheartening to reflect that even today, when we know that eagles have a negligible effect on grouse stocks and lamb numbers and that there is no case at all for persecuting them, the welfare of so many pairs rests on the whims of such unenlightened people. I find it sadder still that so many can blandly say that persecution just doesn't happen, or can turn a blind eye to what goes on on their estates. The real enemy of the Golden Eagle is ignorance, or the prejudice that grows from it.

The Golden Eagle, its nest, eggs and young are fully protected by law, and even if the maximum penalties for contraventions are still too low this legislation is in the main excellent—on paper. Having a good law and enforcing it are two different matters. It is not possible to give the Golden Eagle more than token protection, mainly because its population is thinly scattered over huge areas. The costs involved, not to mention the manpower required to do the job properly, would be astronomical. The solution lies in creating a more sympathetic climate of opinion and a better understanding of the birds. But while many people are working towards this end in a number of ways, the slaughter goes on.

Each year, adult and immature eagles are shot, both at and away from the nest. Others are trapped and die a lingering death in the steel jaws of gin traps illegally set in the open and sometimes deliberately placed to catch eagles and other birds of prey. It is still legal to use the gin trap in Scotland, as long as it is set under cover, although it has long been outlawed south of the Border. A favourite (and wholly illegal) ploy is to place a gin trap on a pole or fence post, just the sort of place a bird of prey or an owl might use as a vantage-point: it then becomes a pole trap. Although pole traps are still widely used, few eagles are caught in them. The same cannot be said about the smaller birds of prey.

In some areas, nests are destroyed or even burned out, whether or not they contain eggs or young, and young eagles and eggs may also be destroyed by other means. I have known cases of eyries being filled with stones to deter the adults from using them. Another favourite trick is for a keeper or shepherd 'accidentally' to keep the birds off the nest by sitting close to it for hours on end. With many pairs of eagles, one does not have to be very close to keep them off. I know of one case where a pair failed to breed for several successive years when these 'innocent' tactics were employed against them.

Still more eagles die every year because they feed on carrion. In some areas poisoned carcasses are put out to control Foxes—a method which seems to be legal in Scotland—and crows—which is certainly illegal. Such baits are bound to attract both eagles and Buzzards, often with disastrous results; in Wales the very rare Red Kite is yet another victim. Accidental poisoning is bad enough, but there is a growing pile of evidence which suggests that poison baits are laid specifically to kill birds of prey. So here we have yet another problem for Scottish eagles, one which surely requires urgent investigation.

Mention of poisoning inevitably brings to mind the toxic chemicals used as agricultural pesticides and their calamitous side-effects on wildlife, especially predatory animals and birds. The story of how D.D.T. and its various metabolites, all excellent chemicals for their primary purpose, have caused widespread mortality and infertility among birds of prey is now well known. There have been some spectacular declines, notably in the case of the Peregrine. Fortunately, in Britain at least, the whole subject has been examined in great detail and a series of voluntary and mandatory bans or restrictions of most of the substances concerned has led to a general recovery by our raptors in all but a few regions. The Golden Eagle is among the species which teetered on the brink of a population crash, at least in part of Scotland, but is no longer considered to be at risk.

In the early 1960s, Jim Lockie and Derek Ratcliffe found that eagles in a wide area of the Western Highlands were suffering a severe decline in breeding success. Where 72 per cent of the pairs in their study area were successful during the period 1937 to 1960, only a mere 29 per cent reared young in 1961 to 1963. They found that eagles were not hatching eggs or, what was worse in many ways, were actually breaking them in the nest. No natural factor such as a change in food supply could account for this abrupt decline, and when a number of unhatched eggs were subjected to chemical analysis and were found to contain residues of the same chemicals that were affecting Peregrines and other birds of prey elsewhere, it was concluded that chemical contamination was at the root of the problem. The main substance involved was dieldrin, widely used at that time in sheep-dips, which the eagles were ingesting and accumulating in their bodies through their habit of feeding on sheep carrion. It was also found that no simultaneous contamination or decline was evident among eagles in the Eastern Highlands where the birds eat more natural prey and where sheep carrion is an unimportant source of food. Within a few years, dieldrin was withdrawn from use. Lockie, Ratcliffe and Dick Balharry continued to monitor the original study area, and before long were able to report that breeding success had returned to normal.

Last, but by no means least, there are those who rob eagles' nests for reasons which have nothing to do with direct persecution. Every year, a few eaglets disappear into the clutches of unscrupulous falconers or 'bird collectors'—in some cases via local people acting as agents. The Secretary of State for Scotland has the power under the Protection of Birds Acts to grant licences for the taking of young Golden Eagles, but in practice very few licences are issued and then only to bona fide applicants who satisfy the Secretary of State's Advisory Committee that they have a good reason for wanting an eagle. Scottish eagles are known to have gone overseas—illegally exported as well as illegally taken! It is also known that large sums of money change hands—large enough to justify the risk of being caught. Until 1976 the maximum penalty for taking an eagle illegally was £25, a derisory figure; it is now £100, but the signs are that this is no deterrent either. Golden Eagles fetch much greater prices. There are even some people whose interest is in dead eagles—taxidermists who are not particularly worried about the origins of specimens and who likewise rake in enough money to make the whole business thoroughly worth their while. Finally, there are the egg-collectors, whose sole aim is to have a clutch of eggs to gloat over—obviously behind closed doors. All these villains know eagles and eagle country as intimately as many of the birds' most ardent protectors (or have agents in the field who do), and they are particularly hard to catch and bring to book. A few are prosecuted in most years, but many more slip through.

As if all this were not enough, there are still more threats to the birds—ones which are growing with every year that goes by. These are the accidental pressures brought about by man's ever-increasing invasion of some areas of eagle country in search of leisure. There are now several places in the north where the growth of tourism and the ability of people to get into areas which were remote even a decade ago have resulted in declining breeding success by some pairs and the total desertion of traditionally occupied sites by others. Nowhere is this more marked than in Speyside and the western Grampians. There are excellent social and economic reasons why tourism should continue to develop, but all too often one suspects that little regard is given to the impact on some of our rarer or more fragile wildlife.

I think most genuine conservationists would accept the loss of a few pairs of eagles if developments were suitably zoned in popular upland areas. There is after all ample room for tourist amenities to develop, planned in such a way that vulnerable habitats or special wildlife do not suffer on a wide scale. Wildlife is an asset and a tourist attraction and people should be encouraged to see it, understand it and enjoy it. It is also reasonable to expect them to respect it; and if some form of control over their movements is imposed they should regard this as being in a good cause. Some of the finest nature reserves in Britain are in the Scottish Highlands, but I sometimes feel that there is all too little control over what goes on in them (not necessarily the fault of the usually hard-pressed wardens!) and not enough respect for them from the very people for whom they were set up.

A few specialist activities like rock-climbing can also have harmful effects on nesting eagles, but fortunately the climbers themselves are showing concern for the side-effects of their sport and in many cases are only too pleased to carry out their activities away from breeding cliffs when asked to do so. Naturalists and bird photographers, alas, can be the Golden Eagle's worst enemy through their usually innocent and often understandable desire to get to grips with nesting pairs at close quarters. This is particularly true in Galloway, for example, where the very few pairs of eagles are subjected to a fantastic amount of pressure from birdwatchers and, in most years, do well if one of their eyries is successful. If we were able to dispel the myth that to see a Golden Eagle properly you must visit its nest, or to persuade people that a little self-discipline and thought for the birds is called for, we would go a long way towards eradicating this particular menace.

The law has been amended to help with these very problems. It is necessary to have a permit from the Nature Conservancy Council to visit an eagle's eyrie, or one runs the risk of prosecution for 'wilful disturbance'. Separate licences are required by bird photographers wishing to work at a nest, and by ornithologists wishing to ring the birds. Perhaps this legislation *has* helped the Golden Eagle—but I sometimes wonder.

The problems facing the Golden Eagle, then, are many and varied; none of them is particularly easy to solve. Some of them appear to be increasing, too. Nevertheless, the Golden Eagle survives; we think it is possibly holding its own, or declining only very slowly. If this is so, the final question must be 'Why so much fuss about persecution, disturbance and so on when the birds are clearly not in imminent danger of disappearing altogether?' There is a straightforward answer, of course, to do with breaking the law—but that will not do.

I think most people would accept that we have a moral responsibility to look after this rather special member of our avifauna, and not only for aesthetic reasons, good as these may be in themselves. We have a conservation duty to safeguard a bird whose population is of European importance— it is in fact rather more than a special Scottish bird, or even a special British one. We should be aiming towards halting the slow decline which many of us believe is taking place—and we must at all costs prevent its acceleration. Left alone, the Golden Eagle will recolonise some of its old haunts, but it will do so only if it is unmolested where it still breeds today. Where it has already shown signs of recolonising—in northern England, for example—it merits protection and encouragement.

Man has done much to alter the Highland environment, not all of it to the benefit of his own kind or the native wildlife, but in spite of everything much of its essential character remains intact. It would lose a good deal of this character if the Golden Eagle disappeared from it. Our aim, then, should be to ensure that this cannot happen. I for one would like to think that we will succeed in promoting a better understanding of eagles, which in the long term is the only way to keep them with us, and that my grandchildren will be able to see them and enjoy them for their own sake just as much as I have done.

Reading List

Much of the work done on Scottish Golden Eagles has been written up in ornithological journals, but there are useful summaries in the works listed here. Some of the titles are long out of print, but are usually available through public libraries.

Golden Eagles: *The Golden Eagle,* Seton Gordon (Collins, 1955). Now a little out of date, but still the standard work on the species. *Days with the Golden Eagle,* Seton Gordon (Williams & Norgate, 1927). Very readable account of the author's early experiences.

Eagles generally: *Eagles,* Leslie Brown (David & Charles, 1976). Easily the best and most up-to-date book on eagles. *Eagles, Hawks and Falcons of the World,* Leslie Brown and Dean Amadon (Country Life Books, 1968). In two volumes; the most comprehensive account of birds of prey on a world basis, with much background information and detailed sections on all eagle species. *Birds of Prey,* Michael Everett (Orbis, 1976). *Birds of Prey: their biology and ecology,* Leslie Brown (Hamlyn, 1976). Two books on birds of prey generally; background reading and much on various eagle species.

British birds of prey: *British Birds of Prey,* Leslie Brown (Collins, 1976). The most up-to-date and comprehensive work on all species. The chapter on the Golden Eagle is particularly good.

Identification: *Flight Identification of European Raptors,* R. Porter, I. Willis, S. Christensen & B. P. Nielsen (T. & A. D. Poyser, 1974). A new concept in identification books; the best for identifying all European eagles, Buzzards, etc.

General: *The Highlands and Islands,* F. Fraser Darling & J. Morton Boyd (Collins, 1964). The best work on the natural history of eagle country; recommended background reading.